I0190230

Coloring Diva's 50 Stained Glass Mandalas

A Coloring Book for Adults with Inspirational Quotations

Series 2

Tankard and Bax

ISBN-13: 978-88-941228-1-7
ISBN-10:8894122816

Talk to Us

We would love to hear from you and see some of your designs. It's amazing how different the versions can be! So please join us on our Drama Llama Press Facebook page, visit our website www.dramallamapress.com and sign up for the newsletter or wing us an email at info@dramallamapress.com We always reply (if we're not coloring in, of course!)

TO OUR FRIENDS

To our fabulous friends, thank you for your love and support.

CONTENTS

INTRODUCTION

Coloring In for Adults – How Does *That* Work?

Remember when you were a kid and spent hours coloring in? Time just flew by as you scribbled happily away. The magic princess's hair? Blue! That weird goblin thing? Purple and green. Yay! All this alchemy achieved with just a few strokes of your rainbow-hued pencils. Oh what fun you had transforming ponies and pixies, flowers and fairies, monsters and moonscapes!

The wonderful world of adult coloring books aims to do the same thing. It transports you back to a time when cares were few and life was simple. But to keep your grown up brain happy, the designs are far more complex than those you did when you were eight and a half.

You'll be amazed how quickly you calm down once you start coloring in the intricate stained glass designs in this book. Time will stand still once more as you enter the enviable state of flow. You know, the one artists crave and writers long for? It's yours for the taking now.

As a bonus, this is an affordable and healthy pastime. You don't have to buy a billion gizmos and gadgets or wear a special uniform (unless you want to, of course). For less than the price of a lycra leotard you can get some crayons or felt pens and a coloring book and you're good to go.

The Science Bit for the Skeptics

Your nearest and dearest may want to call the men in white coats when they find out you have bought a coloring book. But you can reassure them that there is solid science behind your new-found passion.

Everyone knows that modern life is very stressful for many people. There are so many demands on us these days, it almost makes you long for the simple life in a cave with Stanley the Stegosaurus.

The trouble is that our physiology hasn't adapted fast enough to cope with 21st century living. When our prehistoric predecessors faced stress it was in the form of real hairy, scaly, scary things. If cave people were in danger, they went into a flight-or-fight state. This meant their body was flooded with natural chemicals that, among other things, affected organ function and helped them run faster or battle better. Once they had fled or fought, the chemicals dissipated and they could go back to hemming a dragon skin or fashioning a nice hair slide from some bits of old flint.

The flight-or-fight state is fine if you are actually faced with a physical threat. Your body needs to prepare for genuine danger. But if the "threat" is a missed appointment, a credit card bill or unexpected overtime at work then flight-or-fight is a totally inappropriate response. But our bodies do it anyway, flooding us with adrenaline, norepinephrine and cortisol. And there these chemicals stay, sloshing around, doing us no end of harm. We are stressed, but in a chronic way. Not the way nature intended us to be *at all.*

It's almost impossible to avoid this type of modern stress. What we can do is try to deal with it by giving our minds and bodies the opportunity to relax completely. Ideally, we want our brains in an alpha state to help us rebalance and de-stress. That's where coloring helps. The connection with childhood, gentle, repetitive movements, creativity and clear simple focus all combine to move the brain from busy beta brain to agreeable, abstracted alpha.

If You Like Rules – Here They Are

Quite honestly, you don't need to be taught how to color in a pattern. It'll all come back to you like riding a bike. However here are a few guidelines:

- There are no rules.
- Alcohol based liquid colors might bleed through. Colored pencils are better.
- Background music can help you reach the desired zen state quickly. Baroque music (Bach, Vivaldi) is particularly good for this.
- You don't have to complete a whole design in one sitting. There are no deadlines here!
- Buy a pencil sharpener alongside your colored pencils. Being stressed and looking for a sharp blade is not a good combination.
- From time to time check in on how your body is feeling. Holding your pencil so tightly it snaps, leaving marks on the pages or screaming a bit are all clues you are too tense! Consciously make yourself relax.
- Put a pad of paper or a magazine under the design if you are, despite our advice, using colors that may bleed through or if you are scribbling hard like a maniac, in which case, see above.
- Coloring sessions can be great if you need to solve a problem or make a decision. Think about the problem beforehand. Do some coloring and try not to think about it. Afterwards, you may find the solution appears as if by magic.
- Coloring is a great sleep aid, so try a coloring session before bedtime to help you easily access the Land of Nod.
- It's well known that colors can affect mood. Experiment if you want to. Blues and greens can be calming, violet spiritual and reds and oranges energizing.
- Resist the urge to analyze what you're doing as you go along. This is supposed to be fun for its own sake. Got it?
- Enjoy yourself!

About the Authors

Fiona Tankard and Kathryn Bax are friends and recovering Type A personalities who are fiber artists both living in Tuscany, Italy. Their quest to calm down and chill out has led them to try a number of tools, including the wonderful world of adult coloring books.

They live 10 minutes from one another in the beautiful Casentino Valley, the "Hidden Tuscany" of thick chestnut forests, wild boar, deer on the doorstep and beautiful stone farmhouses and castles dotting the countryside. An area inhabited centuries ago by the Etruscans, it has inspired many artists throughout the ages, and was once home to Saint Francis and Michelangelo.

It is within these surroundings that Fiona Tankard and Kathryn Bax live, each keeping fiber animals to use for their weaving company. Fiona keeps alpacas, and Kathryn keeps Angora goats and Finnsheep. Both ladies are very creative, and love working with color and design.

With will one can do anything.

Samuel Smiles

MANDALA 1

We are all inventors, each sailing out on a voyage of discovery, guided each by a private chart, of which there is no duplicate. The world is all gates, all opportunities.

Ralph Waldo Emerson

MANDALA 2

When you get into a tight place and everything goes against you, till it seems you could not hang on a minute longer, never give up then, for that is just the place and time that the tide will turn.

Harriet Beecher Stowe

MANDALA 3

The only way of finding the limits of the possible is by going beyond them into the impossible.

Arthur C. Clarke

MANDALA 4

Life consists not in holding good cards, but in playing those you hold well.

Josh Billings

MANDALA 5

If the wind will not serve,
take to the oars.
Destitutus ventis, remos adhibe

Latin Proverb

MANDALA 6

Men's best successes come after their disappointments.

Henry Ward Beecher

MANDALA 7

Strong lives are motivated by dynamic purposes.

Kenneth Hildebrand

MANDALA 8

Great spirits have always encountered violent opposition from mediocre minds.

Albert Einstein

MANDALA 9

In every difficult situation is potential value. Believe this, then begin looking for it.

Norman Vincent Peale

MANDALA 10

Believe with all of your heart that you will do what you were made to do.

Orison Swett Marden

MANDALA 11

To find what you seek in the road of life,
the best proverb of all is that which says:
"Leave no stone unturned."

Edward Bulwer Lytton

MANDALA 12

Doubt whom you will, but never yourself.

Christian Nestell Bovee

MANDALA 13

Every artist was first an amateur.

Ralph Waldo Emerson

MANDALA 14

Nothing is worth more than this day.
You cannot relive yesterday.
Tomorrow is still beyond our reach.

Johann Wolfgang Von Goethe

MANDALA 15

I was always looking outside myself for strength and confidence, but it comes from within. It is there all of the time.

Anna Freud

MANDALA 16

In any project the important factor is your belief. Without belief, there can be no successful outcome.

William James

MANDALA 17

Do not wait; the time will never be "just right." Start where you stand.

Napoleon Hill

MANDALA 18

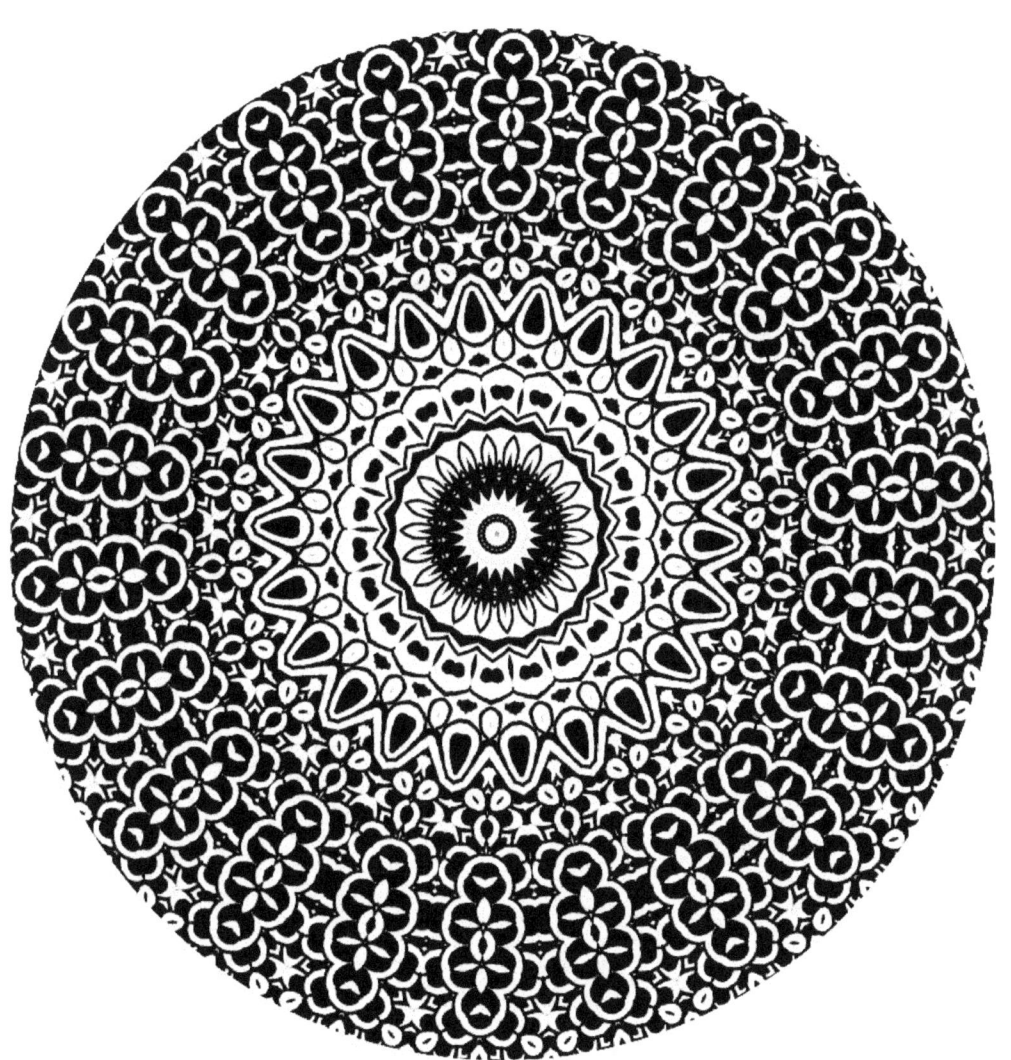

Two men look out the same prison bars; one sees mud and the other stars.

Frederick Langbridge

MANDALA 19

We can do anything we want to do if we stick to it long enough.

Helen Keller

MANDALA 20

I have not the shadow of a doubt that any man or woman can achieve what I have, if he or she will make the same effort, and have the same hope and faith.

Mahatma Gandhi

MANDALA 21

Don't wait for extraordinary opportunities. Seize common occasions and make them great.

Orison Swett Marden

MANDALA 22

No great man ever complains of want of opportunities.

Ralph Waldo Emerson

MANDALA 23

Happy are those who dream dreams and are ready to pay the price to make them come true.

Leon J. Suenes

MANDALA 24

First say to yourself what you would be;
and then do what you have to do.

Epictetus

MANDALA 25

Storms make oaks take roots.

Proverb

MANDALA 26

Nothing contributes so much to tranquilize the mind as a steady purpose--
a point on which the soul may fix its intellectual eye.

Mary Shelley

MANDALA 27

Nothing great was ever achieved without enthusiasm.

Ralph Waldo Emerson

MANDALA 28

We are still masters of our fate.
We are still captains of our souls.

Winston Churchill

MANDALA 29

The journey of a thousand miles begins with a single step.

Lao Tzu

MANDALA 30

What lies behind us and what lies before us are tiny matters compared to what lies within us.

Ralph Waldo Emerson

MANDALA 31

When it is dark enough, you can see the stars.

Persian Proverb

MANDALA 32

You must know for which harbor you are headed if you are to catch the right wind to take you there.

Seneca

MANDALA 33

Regret for the things we did can be tempered by time; it is regret for the things we did not do that is inconsolable.

Sydney J. Harris

MANDALA 34

We must sail sometimes with the wind and sometimes against it, but we must sail, and not drift, nor lie at anchor.

Oliver Wendell Holmes

MANDALA 35

Nothing can stop the man with the right mental attitude from achieving his goal; nothing on earth can help the man with the wrong mental attitude.

Thomas Jefferson

MANDALA 36

The difference between a successful person and others is not a lack of strength, not a lack of knowledge, but rather a lack in will.

Vince Lombardi

MANDALA 37

Welcome every new and difficult problem in life as a new opportunity to wrestle and win — and to gain new experience and new power.

L. H. Murlin

MANDALA 38

Go confidently in the direction of your dreams. Live the life you have imagined.

Henry David Thoreau

MANDALA 39

Every great dream begins with a dreamer. Always remember, you have within you the strength, the patience, and the passion to reach for the stars to change the world.

Harriet Tubman

MANDALA 40

*Reach high, for stars lie hidden in your soul. Dream deep,
for every dream precedes the goal.*

Pamela Vaull Starr

MANDALA 41

The future belongs to those who believe in the beauty of their dreams.

Eleanor Roosevelt

MANDALA 42

The tissue of life to be we weave with colors all our own,
And in the field of destiny we reap as we have sown.

John Greenleaf Whittier

MANDALA 43

Destiny is not a matter of chance; but a matter of choice. It is not a thing to be waited for, It is a thing to be achieved.

William Jennings Bryan

MANDALA 44

The purpose of life is a life of purpose.

Robert Byrne

MANDALA 45

There is only one thing that remains to us, that cannot be taken away: to act with courage and dignity and to stick to the ideals that have given meaning to life.

Jawaharlal Nehru

MANDALA 46

*One way to get the most out of life is
to look upon it as an adventure.*

William Feather

MANDALA 47

The man of wisdom is never of two minds;
the man of benevolence never worries;
the man of courage is never afraid.

Confucius

MANDALA 48

The man who removes a mountain begins by carrying away small stones.

Chinese Proverb

MANDALA 49

To win without risk is to triumph without glory.

Corneille

MANDALA 50

Talk to Us

We would love to hear from you and see some of your designs. It's amazing how different the versions can be! So please join us on our Drama Llama Press Facebook page, visit our website www.dramallamapress.com and sign up for the newsletter or wing us an email at info@dramallamapress.com We always reply (if we're not coloring in, of course!)